MELBOURNE SKETCHBOOK

A memento of Melbourne

from the management

of Heritage & Agriseeds

MELBOURNE SKETCHBOOK

Drawings by
A. ROGER-GENERSH

Text by
BRIAN CARROLL

Published in 1990 by
Loch Haven Books
Arthur's Seat Road, Main Ridge
Victoria 3928
First published as Second Melbourne Sketchbook 1974, Rigby
Revised 1981, Rigby
This revised and expanded edition published 1990
Copyright © A. Roger-Genersh and Brian Carroll 1974
ISBN 1 875308 04 0
All rights reserved
Typeset by Abb-typesetting Pty Ltd, Collingwood, Victoria
Printed by Brown Prior Anderson Burwood, Victoria

CONTENTS

North Melbourne Fountain	6
Victoria Barracks	8
Shrine of Remembrance	10
Simpson and his Donkey	12
Stonnington	14
Adam Lindsay Gordon	16
Pentridge	18
Stanford Fountain	20
157 Hotham Street	22
St Vincent Place	24
South Melbourne Town Hall	26
Trades Hall	28
A Gothic Bank	30
Law Courts	32
Queen Victoria's Statue	34
Terrace Houses	36
Salvation Army Training College	38
Matthew Flinders' Statue	40
City Court	42
Hitching Post	44
Treasury Lamps	46
Separation Tree	48
Royal Terrace	50
Pissoirs	52
Memorial Horse Trough	54
Shot Tower	56
Melbourne Grammar School	58
Melbourne Synagogue	60
Saint Patrick's Cathedral	62

NORTH MELBOURNE FOUNTAIN

"Keep the Pavement Dry" implores one legend on the cast-iron drinking fountain in Errol Street, North Melbourne, outside North Melbourne Town Hall.

The fountain proper is surrounded by quite an imposing circular canopy, richly decorated with cast-iron lace work.

The same pattern can be seen in English country towns, and also in Sydney, Williamstown, and Port Adelaide. A similar model graces the main street of the Riverina town of Hay, and there is an enlarged version in the Launceston Public Gardens.

A close look at the inscriptions on the fountain will show that it was "Presented to the Burgesses by Thomas Henderson, Mayor 1877, Town of Hothan."

In the boom days of the 1850s, the wealth of the colony's gold seemed to make everything possible. As Melbourne spread outwards, the "distant" parts, like North Melbourne, Fitzroy, and Collingwood, felt they should have their own local government.

So a whole series of new municipalites emerged, one of them the Municipality of Hotham. It was created on 30 September 1859 by His Excellency Sir Henry Barkly, and named after his predecessor, Sir Charles Hotham.

The name of the Municipality was changed from Hotham to North Melbourne in 1887. But one school of thought came to believe that Melbourne had been rather too fragmented in the early days. Accordingly, in 1905 the Town of North Melbourne, along with the Borough of Flemington and Kensington, were again incorporated in the City of Melbourne as the Hopetoun Ward, named after Australia's first Governor-General.

VICTORIA BARRACKS

Ability to withstand a Russian bombardment might well have been one reason for the choice of bluestone as the construction material for Victoria Barracks. The job of building them was first put in hand by the Military Works office in 1860.

Red-coated British troops paraded on the barracks square then, and their most likely adversary was a Russian invasion force. In those days, not so long after the Crimean War, Britain still feared a Russian push down through India, even as far as the British colonies in Australia.

In 1870, the Imperial troops went home, leaving Victoria Barracks for Victoria's own artillery, cavalry, and infantry. If the Russians were to come, there would still be somebody to protect the country. There is some evidence that in about 1878 the Russians did have plans for attacking Melbourne in the event of war with Britain.

In 1883, "An Old Colonist" told in a pamphlet of an imaginary Russian invasion of Melbourne. The locals, he said, fought bravely against the 3,000 men who stormed the Heads and landed at Port Melbourne. After a sharp fight for the bridges in the Battle of the Yarra (which was the title of the pamphlet), the victorious Russians departed with a ransom of £3 million.

Scares about Russian invasions went on all through the 1880s. This was the era of Marvellous Melbourne, and it seemed only natural to the proud Melburnians that the Russians should covet such a prize.

But nobody at Victoria Barracks ever did hear the sound of Russian guns—or of any other hostile guns, for that matter.

SHRINE OF REMEMBRANCE

"Let all men know that this is holy ground."
These words, inscribed in bronze on the Shrine of Remembrance, summarise the feeling one gets there. There is also this quote from the ancient Greek poet, Simonides: "This Shrine, established in the hearts of men as on solid earth, commemorates a people's fortitude and sacrifice. Ye therefore that come after, give remembrance."

Public meetings were first held in 1921 to discuss a suitable memorial to men and women who had served in the first World War. An expert committee looked at various locations (twenty were proposed) before the site was chosen on an area known as The Grange. Two Melbourne architects, Hudson and Wardrop, both ex-servicemen, were awarded a prize for the design. It was modelled partly on a monument erected at Halicarnassus in 353 B.C. by Queen Artemesia in memory of her husband, King Mausolus. This was considered to be one of the seven wonders of the ancient world.

Sir John Monash announced the proposal to build the Shrine at a dinner given for the Duke and Duchess of York in 1926. Lord Somers, Governor of Victoria, laid the foundation stone of the central building on Armistice Day, 1927.

So the monument rose slowly on the skyline where it could clearly be seen from any point in Swanston Street and along St Kilda Road, traditional route of the Anzac Day marchers. The Shrine was dedicated by the Duke of Gloucester in 1934, the year of Victoria's centenary. More than 200,000 people watched the ceremony. At the precise hour of 11 a.m. on 11 November, the Duke placed a wreath beside the Stone of Remembrance. "Last Post" and "Reveille" were played, and 10,000 pigeons were released from the upper gallery.

SIMPSON AND HIS DONKEY

Quite close to the Shrine of Remembrance is a smaller, more intimate memorial, a bronze statue of John Simpson Kirkpatick, with his donkey, Murphy.

Their story began late in 1914, when Australian and New Zealand troops, on their way to England, were diverted to Egypt, there to complete their military training. They were soon known as the Australian and New Zealand Army Corps, or A.N.Z.A.C., with General Birdwood in command.

When the British Navy failed to force a passage through the Dardanelles, a land operation was decided upon. On 25 April 1915, Anzac, British, and French troops established a beachhead on the Gallipoli Peninsula against fierce Turkish opposition. For days it seemed quite possible that the invaders would be thrown back into the sea. But they held on grimly, and settled down to months of stalemate.

For the first three weeks, Simpson and his donkey went back and forth between the front line and a clearing station of the Field Ambulance Unit of the Australian Medical Corps. In one direction they carried the wounded. On every return journey they brought badly-needed supplies of drinking water.

Kirkpatrick was only twenty-two when, on 19 May 1915, he and Murphy were killed. The statue makes him one of the few Australian soldiers to have a memorial to himself. The inscription reads: "He Gave His Life That Others Might Live."

It was apparent almost from the start that the Gallipoli campaign must fail, even though it had its moments of triumph. The evacuation was completed on 8 January 1916. In the whole futile exercise Australian dead numbered 8,587, with 19,367 wounded.

STONNINGTON

John Wagner was a businessman who, it seems, never did anything spectacular enough to get his name into the mainstream of Australian history. But he made a sufficient fortune out of investments in the coaching firm of Cobb & Co. and the gold mines of Mount Morgan to build himself a mansion in Glenferrie Road, Malvern.

For his architect he chose C. A. D'Ebro, who had already worked on Princes Bridge, the *Argus* office, Georges, Prahran Town Hall, Prahran Market, and Saint John's Church at Toorak. He chose as his site an area of market gardens and orchards at 336 Glenferrie Road, Malvern. By 1892 Stonnington had been built, and Wagner was installed. He lived there until his death in 1901

About this time the Victorian Government was looking for a residence fitting for the State Governor. They had built a fine Government House near the Botanic Gardens in 1873, but now that Melbourne was the capital of the newly-formed Commonwealth of Australia, that had been taken for the Governor-General.

The Government leased Stonnington, and until some time after the Federal capital moved to Canberra in 1927, it was Victoria's Government House. A succession of governors lived there.

After the governors moved out, Stonnington became successively Saint Margaret's Girls' School, a convalescent hospital for the Australian Red Cross, and an administration centre for the Health Department.

In 1956 it became Toorak State College and later the Toorak Campus of Victoria College.

ADAM LINDSAY GORDON

The sculptured saddle beneath the chair on which Adam Lindsay Gordon sits in Spring Street gives a clue that he was an accomplished horseman as well as a poet. Gordon was virtually exiled from England to Australia after removing a horse from its stable during the night to enter it in a steeplechase the next day.

Twenty-one-year-old Gordon became a police trooper in South Australia, mainly in the Mount Gambier and Penola areas. Here he turned on his most famous piece of horsemanship, the jump across the fence on to the narrow ledge hundreds of feet above Mount Gambier's Blue Lake, followed by the jump out again.

In 1862 he married Margaret Park, only seventeen at the time, and twelve years his junior, but a loving and ideal wife for the young poet, whose first work was published in 1864.

By 1867, when his book of poems *Sea Spray and Smoke Drift* was published, Gordon and his wife were living at Dingley Dell, a house some few miles south of Mount Gambier. They later moved to Ballarat, then to Melbourne.

In Melbourne, Gordon continued to ride successfully, but he fell more than he should, and hurt his head badly on several occasions. Still, he was writing good poetry, notably his book of *Bush Ballads and Galloping Rhymes*, published in 1870.

Then he got news that his lawsuit to establish his claim to the Gordon clan's Scottish estates had been dismissed, leaving him deeply in debt. On 24 June 1870 he simply took his shotgun into the bush near Brighton Beach and killed himself.

PENTRIDGE

In the cemetery at Sale, in Gippsland, there is a headstone "sacred to the memory of Joseph Pentridge, who departed this life on the 7th May 1870, aged 52 years." Thirty years before, the name of this quiet man had been given to a place that was to become notorious for the violent men gathered there.

Joseph Pentridge was nineteen in 1838 when he married Annie, somewhat younger, in the Irish linen-making town of Bainbridge. The newlyweds emigrated to Australia. They first lived in Sydney, but soon moved to Melbourne, by which time they had a daughter, Agnes.

Captain William Lonsdale, Acting Superintendent of the Port Phillip District, employed Pentridge as a book-keeper on his station at Dandenong. Life with the cash book and the journal apparently didn't appeal to the young Pentridge, who headed for the other side of town and squatted on some land near Merri Creek. After a short period there he was off again, this time to Adelaide.

But Pentridge left his name behind for a few weeks after he departed, Superintendent La Trobe gave it to a village that had been laid out on Sydney Road, between four and five miles north of Melbourne. Pentridge Village soon became Pentridge Stockade.

La Trobe's reason for settling his convicts in this spot was simple. There was ample "stone upon the spot, which it [was] proposed that the prisoners should break into metal, for the formation of the main road, both in the direction of the city and in advance upon a line. . ." Hard labour on the roads was a fairly standard sentence in those days.

STANFORD FOUNTAIN

When William Stanford wanted a model for the eagles that were to grace his fountain, it was comparatively easy to arrange for a stuffed eaglehawk to be sent down from Bendigo. But things grew a little more complicated when he needed a nude youth holding a basket of flowers. At the root of Stanford's problem was the fact that he was in Pentridge, having been sent there for twenty years because of his involvement in violence, horse-stealing, and armed robbery. A visiting magistrate finally arranged for a child to come in and be his model, so that the fountain could be finished.

William Walter Tyrell Stanford, alias Walter Tyrrel, alias William Stanford, was born in London in the late 1830s. He was apprenticed to a stonemason, but ran away to sea when his widowed mother remarried. He eventually reached Melbourne and headed for the goldfields.

Convicted of stealing a horse, he was sent to Pentridge for ten years' hard labour, only to be released with a ticket of leave in 1860. But he was soon back in again, this time for twenty years.

In Pentridge, Stanford's talent for sculpture was encouraged. His art developed to such an extent that in time he became engrossed in building his fountain. The only material available to him was the unyielding bluestone of the prison quarry, but after two years of work the fountain was completed.

By now Stanford was quite ill from constantly breathing stone dust. This encouraged agitation for his release, and he was freed on 28 October 1871. His first job on his release was to help erect his fountain in the Gordon Memorial Reserve in Spring Street.

Stanford became successful in business as a monumental mason, but died from "stonemason's disease" in 1880.

157 HOTHAM STREET

East Melbourne is a storehouse of pleasant nineteenth-century houses. One that attracts more interest than most is at 157 Hotham Street.

The *Australian Builder and Railway Chronicle* reported in its issue of 26 January 1861 that "on the south side of [Hotham] street, Mr Reid has designed a picturesque Gothic Villa for the Deputy Surveyor-General, Mr Hodgkinson. It is being built of squared blue stone with white dressings to the quoins and openings. A verandah and balcony extend around the whole of the principal front formed in imitation of carved oak. The roof of the balcony, being a continuation of the main roof, is divided into ornamental gables, the whole giving the appearance of a double front to the building."

It is not certain whether Mr Reid was Joseph Reed, who designed some of Melbourne's larger buildings, including the Town Hall, but the confident way the journal tosses off his name suggests that he may have been.

Clement Hodgkinson, Deputy Surveyor-General, was one of Melbourne's leading citizens during the latter half of the nineteenth century.

Soon after his arrival in Victoria in 1851 he took a job as a draftsman in the Surveyor-General's office, thinking it would be temporary. He eventually worked his way up to Deputy Suerveyor-General, but never quite made it to the top position of Surveyor-General. In 1874, shortly after his management was criticised at a public enquiry, Hodgkinson retired on a pension.

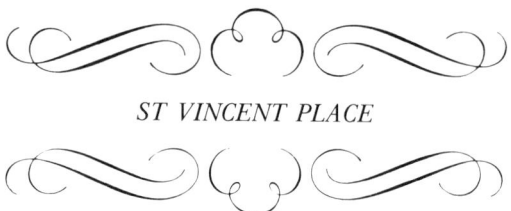

ST VINCENT PLACE

Look at a map of Albert Park, and you will see how the best-laid plans of town-planners such as Clement Hodgkinson can be cut through by railway engineers. St Vincent Gardens and the series of crescents that surround them had their eastern end not too neatly severed by the railway to St Kilda. So the statue of Saint Vincent at the orphanage of Saint Vincent de Paul, in Cecil Street, doesn't quite look down Service Street into St Vincent Gardens in the way it was meant to do.

Perhaps it was proximity to the railway that made St Vincent Place such a desirable address when the first allotments were auctioned there in the 1860s.

When Block 41B was sold on 26 September 1866, four of the ten blocks were bought at an average price of £136 by W. P. Buckhurst, who was deeply involved in the real estate business in South Melbourne, where he became the largest purchaser of Crown Lands. He built Rochester Terrace, 35–51 St Vincent Place, one of the grandest terraces in Melbourne.

Number 9 St Vincent Place stands on a block of land originally sold to D. Simpson. There is no entry in the rate book for Simpson, so he must have sold it almost immediately to James Leggatt. The house, built in the late 1860s, was purchased in the 1870s by Josiah Marks, an insurance broker, whose family lived there for decades.

Over the years, the fine houses of St Vincent Place became more than a little run-down. But like many such spots, it has had its renaissance, and most of the houses are showing again that somebody loves them.

SOUTH MELBOURNE TOWN HALL

Soon after the Town of Emerald Hill (as South Melbourne was originally known) had been set up under the Municipal Corporations Act of December 1854, the city fathers began to think of building a splendid town hall.

Unfortunately the orphan asylum occupied the prime central block in the town. Council suggestions that the asylum should go elsewhere began in 1856 and finally bore fruit in 1877, when an Act of Parliament banished the orphanage to Brighton, awarding it £90,000 compensation for the site.

Charles Webb designed an imposing town hall, elaborately ornamented, with six fluted Corinthian columns on the portico, a graceful spire rising from its centre, and the coat of arms of the municipality on the tympanum.

John Boyd, Mayor of Emerald Hill, performed the ceremony of commencement of building at 4 p.m. on 27 March 1879, the contract having been awarded to Gillon and Treeby. Some 300 guests attended the dinner which followed.

It was not the friendliest of dinners. In the aftermath of a second deadlock between the Legislative Assembly and the Legislative Council, tempers frayed easily. According to the *Argus*, when the chairman proceeded to call on someone to propose the next toast, "he was not allowed to proceed until he had given the assurance that Mr Service [representing the Opposition] would speak in a few minutes."

A grand ball was held on 1 July 1880 to celebrate the opening of the new town hall.

TRADES HALL

Benjamin Douglas, a great Trade Unionist, headed the 1856 delegation which asked the Victorian Government for land for a trades hall. The government responded with a grant of one acre at the corner of Victoria and Lygon streets, and by 1859 a primitive wooden building had been erected there.

But grand ideas were afoot in gold-rush Melbourne of the middle 1800s, and most people were building in a style to fit the mood. The workers, seeing no reason to be left out, chose one of the colony's leading architects, Joseph Reed, to design them a fine trades hall. Reed's other work included Melbourne Town Hall, the Independent Church, Scots Church, the Public Library, the Museum, the Art Gallery, Ormond College, the Exhibition Building, and the University's original Wilson Hall.

Work on the Trades Hall eventually started in January 1874, but the project was hardly rushed. In 1888, *The Picturesque Atlas of Australia* recorded that "when completed, it will have cost something like ten thousand pounds, and will nearly cover the acre of ground granted by the Legislature for its perpetual use."

The year in which the Trade Union movement took its first step towards establishing the Trades Hall was also the year in which it managed to establish the principle of the eight-hour day. In February 1856, Melbourne's stonemasons decided that after 24 March they would work only eight hours a day, which in the standard six-day week of the time meant a forty-eight-hour week. Most employers were receptive to the idea. A delay was agreed upon, so that all the other tradees could get themselves equally well-organised. On 21 May 1856, to celebrate their victory, the unions marched joyfully through the streets of Melbourne.

A GOTHIC BANK

The Gothic style, while popular for cathedrals and churches, never quite caught on for Melbourne's secular buildings. One exception is all the more unique for that.

Sir George Verdon, K.C.M.G., general manager of the English, Scottish, and Australian Chartered Bank Limited, undoubtedly took a keen interest in the building that was to be erected on the corner of Collins and Queen streets, in the heart of Melbournes's financial district, in the 1880s. Two of its three floors were to be his residence, while the ground floor would provide offices and a banking chamber.

The architect was William Wardell, who, before emigratting to Australia in 1858, had been a disciple of Pugin, the well-known Gothic revivalist in England. Wardell's first Melbourne commission was Saint Patrick's Cathedral. Directors of the bank announced Wardell's designs in 1883. The *Illustrated Australian News* of 3 October 1883 described the proposed style as fourteenth century English Gothic.

On completion, however, the building clearly displayed the influence of Venetian Gothic. Its sturdy columns, the contrast betweenthe flat stone walls and rich decoration, the loggias and small balconies, and the absence of vertical features have no resemblance to English Gothic. They are, however, strongly reminiscent of the Palazzio Ca D'Oro (1430) and to a lesser extent the Doge's Palace (1309-1425), both in Venice.

The banking chamber, with its extraordinarily rich decoration, forms an extreme contrast to the somewhat austere exterior.

LAW COURTS

When a Royal Commission decided in 1871 that it was high time Melbourne had law courts befitting such a city, nobody was too surprised. Informed people had been saying that since the early 1850s, when Melbourne's first population explosion began. In 1863 a parliamentary select committee proposed the building of new law courts "with as little delay as possible."

The Royal Commission asked that the new building should be "of simple character, and built of brickwork rendered in Portland cement outside." Given the grandness of Melbourne's earlier building sprees, it was a miserly request, which the architects and builders fortunately chose to ignore.

They elected not a simple style, but a "modern Italian" design replete with Ionic and composite columns. And for the outside facing they used not Portland cement but Tasmanian freestone.

First there was a design competition, won in May 1873 by architect Alfred Louis Smith. Unfortunately, word got out that Arthur Ebden Johnson, the Public Works Department man who sat in judgement on the entries, was rather too friendly with Smith. In fact, the winning entry was the joint effort of Smith and Johnson. Johnson was suspended from his post, and Smith's award was withdrawn.

In time it was decided that Smith's design really was the best, and that there had been nothing of a "corrupt or pecuniary interest" in Johnson's involvement with him.

The contract for the foundations was let in August 1874, and gradually the building began to rise at the corner of William and Lonsdale streets. The first proceedings in the new Law Courts were held on 15 February 1884.

QUEEN VICTORIA'S STATUE

On 24 May 1907, Queen Victoria's birthday, 10,000 Melbourne people gathered on a hill near Alexandra Avenue to see Lieutenant-Governor Sir John Madden unveil a statue in her honour.

It was a memorial given by a loving and devoted people to a noble monarch's most noble reign, he said. "She came to a kingdom and left it an empire, built by peace and not bloodshed." Countless hundreds of thousands of dead Africans, Australian Aborigines, Indians, Maoris, and Boers might have disputed that last claim, but there is no record that they were represented at the function.

The idea of a statue of Queen Victoria had been broached in Melbourne even before the obsequies following her death had been performed. The Lieutenant-Governor and the Mayor had decided to invite subscriptions towards the £10,000 estimated to be needed for the project. Melbourne, so they thought, was probably the only city of such a size in the whole British Empire without a statue of Queen Victoria. This was hardly fitting, since the state had been named after her, and its capital after her first prime minister.

As things turned out, £10,000 was not enough. The finished job cost £12,346. Edinburgh-born John White, who had come to Australia while a young man, was chosen to execute the commission.

He sculpted Queen Victoria from Carrara marble, and chose to depict her in her ceremonial robes, complete with Imperial orb and sceptre. A potted life story is shown on the sides of the supporting base in four succinct statements: Birth 1819, Reign 1837–1901, Marriage 1840, Death 1901. The inscription plaques incorporate symbolic figures of Progress, History, Wisdom, and Justice.

TERRACE HOUSES

There seems to be no reason why, in a country as big and as empty as Australia, and so long before suburban sprawl was bothersome, people should need to build terrace houses.

There are at least two explanations. Some wanted their new country to be as much as possible like the old, so they tried to build a mini-England down under. London had terrace houses; so should Melbourne.

Others built from less noble motives. In the rush for riches that characterised much of nineteenth-century Melbourne, terrace houses enabled the shrewd property-owner to squeeze as many buildings as possible on any one piece of land.

One definition of a terrace house, from David Saunders, is that it is "a house with blind boundaries, gaining light and air from windows at the front and rear." Frequently, identical terrace houses were built in a row, but in many rows individualism held full sway. This house, in Nicholson Street, Fitzroy, is so individual that it even rises an extra storey above its fellows.

With their wealth of decoration, particularly of cast and wrought iron, and cement plaster knobs of one kind and another, the terrace houses of the inner and near suburbs gave Melbourne much of its charm. But they slowly slipped out of favour, until some councils in 1918 and 1920 actually banned them.

By the 1960s they were back in fashion. People were industriously restoring the old ones and busily building modern new ones, which they preferred to call "town houses."

SALVATION ARMY TRAINING COLLEGE

From its Australian beginnings in Adelaide in 1880, the Salvation Army soon spread to other parts of the country. More trained officers were needed, so in 1883 training was commenced, at Prahran at first, with three cadets. Several other locations were used until a permanent training site was found.

With the coming Federation of the colonies, the Army began to think of a Federal Training Garrison. A suitable property, running from Victoria Parade to Albert Street, was bought for £4,500.

The red brick, Scottish baronial style building, with cement facings and three battlemented towers, is said to have been the idea of Commandant Herbert Booth, then the Army leader in Australia, and son of the founder.

Earl Hopetoun, the first Governor-General, was to perform the opening ceremony on 16 July 1901, but because he was ill at the time, the Countess took his place. During his address Commandant Booth spoke of the desire to "Evangelise the Archipelago."

Of the 2,000 people who gathered for the ceremony, most had come to see the Countess hoist the flag. But there was also one Fleming, a noted Red-flag orator, who took advantage of the ready-made crowd. Meanwhile, in the portico of the Free Thought Hall, on the opposite side of the road, a noisy band did its best to interrupt proceedings. Still, the Salvation Army was used to a little banter, and amid alternate volleys of hooting and cheering the flag went up.

The building was used to train cadets until 1980, when it was sold to a consortium of architects.

MATTHEW FLINDERS' STATUE

Flinders brought H.M.S. *Investigator* in through Port Phillip Heads on 26 April 1802. Six days was all he could spare for exploring the bay, since his provisions were running low. *Investigator* had sailed from England via the Cape, making slow progress as her master explored Australia's southern coast.

On the morning after their arrival, Flinders and "some other gentlemen" climbed to the top of Arthur's Seat, where they spent much of the day. Across the bay, on the western shore, they met some friendly Aborigines, with whom they exchanged presents and shared lunch.

Flinders sailed away on 3 May 1802, congratulating himself on making a new and useful discovery. On his arrival in Sydney he learnt that Acting Lieutenant John Murray had sailed *Lady Nelson* into the bay on 15 February 1802, less than three months before.

Flinders liked what he had seen around the bay. He wrote: "The country surrounding Port Phillip has a pleasing, and in many parts a fertile appearance, and the sides of some of the hills and several of the vallies, are fit for agricultural purposes. It is in great measure a grassy country and capable of supporting much cattle, though better calculated for sheep."

He was less enthusiastic about the harbour itself. It might hold a lot of ships, but the entrance was dangerously narrow, and certain combinations of wind and tide could make it disastrous for small ships.

Web Gilbert, who created the statue of Flinders, first won world recognition with his nine-metre-high statue of an Australian soldier, erected at Mont St Quentin, as a tribute to Australians who died in France and Belgium in the first World War.

CITY COURT

From Melbourne's earliest days there have been court buildings on the corner of Russell and La Trobe streets. The first modest stone building was erected there in 1842-43, an inelegant two-storey Gothic edifice facing Lonsdale Street. To cope with the sudden surge of court work in the gold-rush days, a flimsy wooden extension was added in 1853.

Everybody seemed to be agreed on the need for a new court. But in the rash of public building that went on in the 1850s, Melbourne never seemed to get around to replacing the "picturesque ruins" where the colony's evil-doers faced the forces of law and order.

Some famous trials were held there. In 1855, thirteen prisoners taken at the Eureka Stockade were arraigned for high treason, "to depose our Lady the Queen from the kingly name and her Imperial Crown," as the charge expressed it. The only convictions to arise from these trials put two spectators in gaol for a week. Chief Justice A'Beckett took exception to their cheering in court when the first of the defendants was acquitted. Henry Seekamp, editor of the *Ballarat Times*, was less fortunate. He was gaoled for sedition, but released after three months.

When Ned Kelly went on trial in 1880 Melbourne was still making do with its ramshackle set of court buildings at the corner of Russell and Lonsdale streets.

Supreme Court sittings moved to the new Law Courts after 1884, but the Russell Street buildings survived until 1910, when they were demolished to make way for the new City Court. This was completed in 1911 to the plans of Mr Austin, an architect with the Public Works Department, which elected to use Australian materials throughout. Yellow stone for the exterior came from Moorabool, and marble from Gippsland.

HITCHING POST

People who visit Bouverie Street these days rarely have need of a hitching post. But they would have done back in 1858, when Rosenberg and Company opened their North Melbourne Brewery there.

John Bellman took over these premises as the Carlton Brewery in 1864. Bellman did not prosper, and the business was purchased by Edward Latham and G. M. Milne. Latham, who succeeded in establishing Carlton Brewery on a sound footing, is usually regarded as its founder.

His company was destined to dominate the Melbourne brewing scene, for in 1907 it was joined by M'Cracken's City Brewery, Victoria Parade Brewery, Castlemaine Brewery, Shamrock Brewery, and Foster's Brewery, to become Carlton and United Breweries Limited.

The Foster brothers came from New York in 1888 and gave the local brewers a rough time by concentrating on bottled beer. Castlemaine Brewery joined from a position of less strength. During 1902 microbes and bacteria had got into their South Melbourne plant, and the resulting bad brews had tarnished their product's image.

The merger involved virtually a dozen breweries, some of the six partners themselves being the product of earlier mergers.

But such high corporate considerations would not have bothered any of the countless horses that must have stood tethered to the Bouverie Street hitching post.

The bluestone buildings into which their owners disappeared are a mixed lot, having grown up as the brewery expanded. The office block on the corner of Bouverie and Victoria streets is of much later origin than those around it, having replaced a hotel that occupied the site.

TREASURY LAMPS

The high-branched cast-iron lamps outside the Treasury Building were not part of the original design of John James Clark, who was only nineteen when he signed the plans and was acknowledged as architect of Melbourne's most elegant building.

The lamps came in 1867, five years after completion of the Italian Renaissance style Treasury, built in Bacchus Marsh sandstone on bluestone foundations.

Melbourne was accustomed to getting its street lighting as an afterthought. In its early days the only outdoor illumination had come from the occasional oil lamp hung outside a shop door.

Hotels and places of entertainment were soon required to provide lamps outside their premises. This had the dual effect of lighting the streets, while attracting people to the pubs and theatres like moths to a candle.

By the middle 1840s the town council was planning to light the main streets, and a few "miserable dark lanterns" began to appear. Night and morning the lamplighter went his rounds, on foot at first, but eventually by bicycle. Oil gave way to gas, and gas to electricity. In time the Treasury lamps were themselves converted to electricity.

Replacement of the Treasury lamps with streamlined modern types seems unlikely. But they do have their problems. Rust is their main enemy. And the fact that every piece of glass in them is a different size is no help at all when a piece occasionally needs replacement.

SEPARATION TREE

Not far from the Botanic Gardens entrance gate, near the Anderson Street bridge, is a red gum that stood there long before John Batman chose the spot for his village.

A plaque on the old gum declares: "Under this tree on the 15th November, 1850, the citizens of Melbourne rejoiced on the receipt of the news that Victoria was to become a separate colony."

Some rejoicing was only to be expected. Agitation for severance of the Port Phillip District from New South Wales had been going on almost since the earliest settlers had stepped ashore.

The first Separation Committee was formed in 1840. This was the beginning of nearly a decade of meetings, petitions, and argument about the subject. There had even been a separation banquet in Melbourne in 1846, but due to a change of government in England it proved to be a little premature.

Finally, on 5 August 1850, Queen Victoria signed the Australian Colonies Government Act, a portmanteau Bill. One provision of the Act was that, as from 1 July 1851, the Port Phillip District would be separated from New South Wales, and would become the Colony of Victoria.

The news reached Melbourne with the arrival of the *Lysander* on Monday 11 November 1850. The rest of the week was declared a holiday. That night an enormous pile of timber on Flagstaff Hill was set alight as a pre-arranged signal to spread the good news, and to start widespread rejoicing.

ROYAL TERRACE

Those who built Royal Terrace in 1854 obviously did not share the jerry-built, quick-profit philosophy of most builders of gold-rush Melbourne. They went in for size and grace when most people had scant regard for these qualities.

Some socially prominent citizens consequently saw fit to make their home in one of the ten three-storey houses that lie within its bluestone outer walls.

John O'Shanassy was one of them. Already a citizen of the Port Phillip District for fifteen years before Royal Terrace was built, this Irish immigrant had been a grazier, draper, and politician. He was appointed to Victoria's first Legislative Council in 1851, and was Premier of Victoria three times: in 1857, in 1858–59, and in 1861–63.

Another resident was painter Nicholas Chevalier. After his arrival in Melbourne in 1855, Chevalier became the first cartoonist of Melbourne *Punch*, an occupation that kept him busy making fun of O'Shanassy's cronies and opponents for a while. Chevalier spent more than ten years in Melbourne, painting a steady stream of Australian landscapes.

Dr Louis Lawrence Smith lived at Number 6 Royal Terrace. His specialty was his mail-order medical business. A letter outlining your symptoms brought back a speedy diagnosis and prescription for treatment. Always providing, of course, that you sent the necessary one pound note with your letter. Smith's discreet service probably had special appeal for those who thought they might have picked up a social disease.

Dr Smith became so prosperous that he outgrew Royal Terrace and moved into the top end of Collins Street, where for decades Melbourne's more expensive doctors continued to practise.

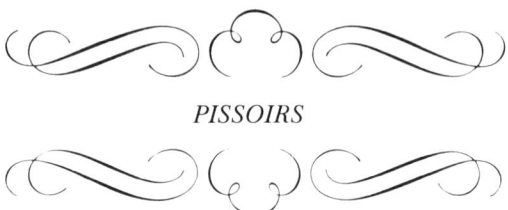

PISSOIRS

Nothing escapes the attention of the National Trust. It classified the men's cast-iron urinal that formerly stood at the corner of Exhibition and Lonsdale streets as "C"—Notable: worthy of preservation.

The citation described it as "a standard two-bay cast-iron urinal of 1908, constructed of patterned panels between slotted uprights and with crested iron top plate, evocative of an age when the artistic impulse graced even the humblest aspects of daily life."

Similar pissoirs are still to be found at the corner of Albert and Nicholson streets and the corner of Flinders and Exhibition streets.

Most examples of Melbourne's cast-iron adornment had a less practical application, although it was commonly used in fences and gates, balustrades, and street furniture, as well as in purely decorative ways, such as verandah friezes.

Melbourne's earliest examples of cast-iron building materials were imported, but local manufacture soon became an important industry. Cast-iron lent itself to repetitive processes, so it was comparatively inexpensive, an important consideration in the days when so much of our building was done by the common man for the common man, and in a hurry at that.

The techniques used to produce cast-iron lace meant that the work of an artist could be reproduced many times. In the casting operation, the pattern (made from kauri pine, cedar, or redwood) was pressed down in a mixture of sand and clay in a shallow box. Another box of clay and sand was pressed down on this. The boxes were separated so that the pattern could be removed, then they were pegged together again, and the hollow space was filled with molten pig-iron.

MEMORIAL HORSE TROUGH

Horses for the British Army in India were an early export from Australia. Later, Australia began to export its men as well as its horses to fight in other people's wars.

The first time Melbourne saw its sons, husbands, and lovers go off *en masse* to an overseas war was at the close of the nineteenth century. In South Africa, some Boers had seen fit to insult the Empire. Melbourne followed the news of the war closely, celebrating such victories as the Relief of Mafeking and Ladysmith. In time most of the men came back, but quarantine considerations meant that the horses had to stay behind. Some of the Australians, it was said, shot their faithful mounts rather than have them fall into unknown hands.

Men and horses fought bravely enough in South Africa, but the British generals bungled things so badly that the Kaiser felt encouraged to take them on within little more than a decade. The streets of Melbourne again resounded to the clatter of hoofs and the jangle of accoutrements, as men and horses headed for the waiting transports.

The Australian Light Horse made its name in the deserts of the Middle East, where the Turk was the enemy. Australian cavalry took part in the brilliant outflanking movement that led to the capture of Damascus.

In time the men came home, but again the horses stayed. Somebody saw fit to remember them with a horse trough in St Kilda Road, inscribed with this verse:

> He gains no crosses as a soldier may,
>   No medals for the many risks he runs;
> He only in his puzzled patient way
>   Sticks to his guns.

SHOT TOWER

A Bristol mechanic named Watts, so the tradition goes, spent all day cutting up strips of lead to make shot, then imbibed rather freely before going to bed. In his troubled sleep, he dreamed the skies were raining molten lead. Strangest of all, he noticed, each piece as it cooled turned into a small sphere. From his dream the idea of the shot tower was born.

Walter Coop's family business in pipes and metal sheets had begun in Melbourne in the 1850s, and between 1888 and 1891 the firm built a shot tower for the manufacture of lead shot. This tower can still be seen from the steps of the Museum in Swanston Street.

The new structure was sufficiently interesting for the *Australian Illustrated News* to send two of its staff there, "one armed with pencil and sketch book, the other with the notebook of the scribe." Their report appeared in the issue of 1 December 1891.

Lead went up the 50 metre tower in ingots. On the upper levels it was melted and poured into a colander-like vessel. Molten metal poured through the perforations and began the long fall down the tower. The single stream gradually broke up and the resulting drops became cooler and rounder before finally reaching the pool at the bottom.

Here the shot was shovelled up, at the rate of six tons a week, and taken to the separating tables. A series of sieves sorted the good round shot from that which had to be recycled, and the good shot into sizes. The noise of this operation was deafening, but for many years now the shot tower itself has been silent.

MELBOURNE GRAMMAR SCHOOL

Some of Melbourne's more notable citizens assembled on 30 July 1856 to see Bishop Perry lay the foundation stone for a Church of England Grammar School to accommodate 400 pupils. The building was to be both spacious in extent and ornate in character. Three of its façades were to "possess considerable pretensions to architectural beauty."

The Reverend John Edward Bronley opened the school on 7 April 1858 with twenty-four boarders and fifty-three day boys. Melbourne Grammar quite soon had its quota of interesting pupils and old boys. When Alfred Vincent Chick entered the school in 1861 he had already served as a powder monkey at the siege of Lucknow four years before, during the Indian Mutiny.

The Witherby Tower, which completed the south front, was financed in 1876 by Arthur Witherby as a mark of gratitude for the care and attention given his son by the then headmaster, Mr Morris. Hubert Witherby had come to Melbourne "seeking health under a brighter sky." But he was not to find it, and died in spite of the efforts of Mr Morris.

The first-ever game of Australian Rules Football was played between teams from Melbourne Grammar and Scotch College, on 7 August 1858. But at least one master there did not approve of it. Gustav Techow, a graduate of the Ling Gymnastic Institute of Stockholm, supervised physical training at the school from 1862 to 1863 and from 1883 to 1887. Football as played in Melbourne in the 1860s was, he said, "devoid of all those features which should characterise the games of a civilised nation."

MELBOURNE SYNAGOGUE

When members of the Melbourne Hebrew Congregation gathered on 14 April 1929 to witness the laying of the foundation stone of their new synagogue, they saw a bottle containing records placed beneath the stone. Only the day before, this bottle had been recovered from under the foundation stone of the old synagogue in Bourke Street, laid in 1853.

When the first immigrant ship, the *Hope*, arrived from England in 1839, it brought some people of the Jewish faith. A government grant of a block of land in Bourke Street in 1844 enabled a synagogue to be built. Erected at a cost of £270, it was only six metres by nine metres and just over five metres high.

With the influx of people that the gold rush brought, that first synagogue proved to be inadequate. Architect Charles Webb designed a new one; its foundation stone was laid on 1 December 1853. The bottle of records was placed beneath it. The new synagogue was consecrated in April 1855. Like most of Melbourne's early places of worship, it was pressed into service even before its interior was completed. For the first year, its walls were hung with calico.

In 1927 the site was sold to the Equity Trustees Company. The synagogue was demolished and replaced by a six-storey office block.

Nahum Barnet was architect for the new synagogue at the corner of St Kilda and Toorak roads. He gave it a classical style, with Corinthian columns to its handsome portico, and a copper dome a full chain in diameter. Inside there is space for 1,300 persons—men downstairs, ladies upstairs, in the Jewish fashion.

SAINT PATRICK'S CATHEDRAL

To cater for Catholics on the east side of Melbourne, Father Geoghegan asked for and was granted land there in 1848. A wooden chapel and two half-finished stone churches succeeded it in the next ten years. In 1848, James Alipius Goold was appointed Catholic Bishop of Melbourne over Father Geoghegan. He formed a Catholic Association to raise money for churches and schools, of which Saint Patrick's was without a doubt to be the most massive.

William Wardell was already an accomplished designer of Roman Catholic churches when he arrived in Melbourne in 1858. Saint Patrick's was his first commission in his new environment.

He designed his cathedral around some existing pillars meant for the smaller church already under construction. That limitation does not seem to have inhibited the grandeur of his concept, which is liberal in its use of flying buttresses, pinnacles, and turrets. Inside, Saint Patrick's is an essay in massive simplicity, produced by the height and dimensions of the clustered columns that support the arches of the naves, and the superb marble altars.

The nave has been in use since 1869, the transepts and central tower were begun in 1870, and the Lady Chapel was built in 1879. Saint Patrick's had to wait a long time for the three towers and spires designed by Wardell. They were finally added, along with the west portal, between 1936 and 1939. But they were thirty metres higher than Wardell had planned them eighty years before.

The severity of bluestone was relieved with white freestone, from Sydney and Hobart, in the door and window surrounds, inner arches, decorative work both inside and out, and in the groining of the aisles.